# Patience Perseverance Prayer
## A Devotional for Entrepreneurs

J. Russell Fugett

# Dedication

To the women whose faith, prayers, and patience set an example and whose courageous faith in me and God's work in my life made this text possible: My wife, Selah, my mother, Anne Payne Fugett, my grandmother Carolyn Cooper Fugett.

I love you.

To the men who poured into me in different seasons of my faith journey: George Sanker, Michael Tapscott, Pastor Bruce Clark, Bishop Glenn Kauffman.

I thank you.

To my late grandfather, J. Howard Payne Jr., who taught me to kneel and pray.
To my late grandfather, Jean S. Fugett, Sr.,  who showed me how to love and serve without complaint.
To my late grandmother, Natalie K. Payne, who exemplified endurance and perseverance unto God's promise.

I remember you.

To my father, Jean S. Fugett Jr., and godfather Abner Haynes, who taught me so many business lessons, people lessons, and the importance and power of understanding life in a spiritual context.

I honor you.

Thank you to my mother Anne, mother Pam Kaye, and wife for reviewing and editing this text.
Thank you to Stephanie Lindo for designing the cover, overseeing print and digital production and helping get this project over the finish line.
Thank you!

# Introduction

I began writing this devotional in 2012, but lacked the faith to immediately follow through. Perhaps this sounds familiar if you're an entrepreneur. Every idea has a season in God's timing (Ecclesiastes 3), but it's easy to talk ourselves out of taking the first step and allowing God to order the steps to follow.

There are always reasons to doubt and allow our imagination to run wild with all of the ways we could fail, embarrass ourselves, and lose time and money. Amidst the cycle of business ups and downs and trying to make ends meet, it was difficult to see how I could possibly follow through on what I knew God was calling me to do in writing this book. To the Christian entrepreneur, this should sound familiar. Starting and running our own enterprise is particularly grueling. I'd ask myself, when will I possibly have time to respond to God's call? Eventually, I came to realize that this journey and who the journey was making me into as a man was the most important thing. I learned that by focusing on everything God had called me to, I would grow into the reality of what I envisioned when I first felt led to begin writing this book.

I realized that a transformation (Romans 12:2) in my thinking would be key to future success and to gaining wisdom and insight; the wisdom and insight that I will share with you in the pages that follow. Was the journey painful? Yes. Growth does not come without sacrifice. There is often pain in gaining enlightenment but, through Christ all things are redeemable if we stay the course (Romans 8:18). I thank God for sending people and provision that have allowed me to stay this course and gain a depth of clarity and understanding I could've only imagined five years ago, let alone ten years ago when I formed my first company. I look forward to what God has to teach me in these next ten years. I hope to continue to have the chance to share it with others so that more of us may be empowered to build businesses that bless and empower people and innovate and create in a way that meets the many critical needs of this time. Thank you for reading this text. Be encouraged!!!

# Day 1

## Discovering The Best Business Partner Ever

*But seek first his kingdom and his righteousness, and all these things will be given to you as well.*

*Matthew 6:33 (NIV)*

The most powerful revelation that I've had as a entrepreneur is that Father God is my business partner. Like in any significant relationship, maintaining communication, and understanding the direction the Father is taking us, on a daily basis, is key. A venture birthed through prayer and properly aligned ambition will not fail in the eyes of God. And yes, we will come to learn that God's perspective is the only one that matters. It's hard to not compare ourselves to other entrepreneurs. We must turn off social media and stop comparing ourselves to the crowd. Our Lord has a plan for us and in order for us to discover that, we must press into Him and welcome His presence into our lives and into our ventures. By doing this, we will have something much more valuable than success as defined by the world. We will have peace that surpasses all understanding and we will have a relationship with Christ that will allow us to truly move mountains!

**Prayer**
*Father, help me to know that You are my first and most important business partner and that through a relationship with You, You will order my steps and see to it that my enterprise flourishes unto Your glory.*

# Day 2

## Being Equally Yoked in Business

*Do not be yoked together with unbelievers. For what do righteousness and wickedness have in common? Or what fellowship can light have with darkness? What harmony is there between Christ and Belial ? Or what does a believer have in common with an unbeliever?*

*2 Corinthians 6:14-15 (NIV)*

Values matter. In any organization, enterprise, or family unit there must be shared values. Values are defined as "a person's principles or standards of behavior; one's judgment of what is important in life." If Christ is at the center, then principles, standards, and judgement should be in sync with Christ. Of course, we are all at different places in our walk and we all have unique struggles, but the key is that we are all walking in the same direction: towards a deeper and more intimate relationship with Christ.

If this relationship is truly the object of our pursuit as a leader, then we must partner with those who are similarly walking the walk. A business partnership is truly a marriage. Families become dependent on each other for survival. If God is in it, our businesses should be meeting a critical need, while also blessing our lives and that of our partners. Partnerships can impact the kinds of clients we serve and the ability to stay true to the mission and vision we believe God gave us for our organizations. Why have partners who will not support that mission and vision? We should prayerfully choose our business partners. Remember some marriages look good on paper, and by the world's standards, but will not give us peace and will impede what God has for us in our businesses.

**Prayer**
*Lord, teach me to be discerning in selecting partners in my venture and to not be seduced by potential, but, instead, seek to prayerfully discern spiritual alignment.*

# Day 3

## Managing Our Expectations of Fellow Christians Entrepreneurs.

*Out of his fullness we have all received grace in place of grace already given.*

*John 1:16 (NIV)*

Many of us in the Church are frustrated and disappointed by other Christians. Often this is because we have higher expectations of our fellow Christians than we have of non-Christians. Recently my firm submitted a proposal to support the operations of another Christian business owner. This was someone I had known for four years and someone whose walk I had witnessed bear fruit. After two intake meetings that included a strategy session, we submitted our proposal. I had to text to confirm they received our proposal and I never received a formal response. "How ungrateful and rude!" I thought. "I deserve better and as a Christian, why would they treat me that way even if their response was thanks but no thanks." My wife had to pull me back from the ledge, help me to take myself out of it and apply grace to the situation. We communicated eventually and our time to work together will probably come. But I almost didn't follow up and could have lost any chance to do business with this person down the line. So apply grace and perhaps consider giving a double dose to those walking this faith journey of entrepreneurship.

**Prayer**
Lord, help me to extend grace to people in the marketplace regardless of their affiliation, understanding we all ultimately fall short.

# Day 4

## If God Is Ordering My Steps, Why Does It Seem Like I'm Going In Circles?

*The Lord makes firm the steps of the one who delights in him; though he may stumble, he will not fall, for the Lord upholds him with his hand.*

*Psalm 37:23-24 (NIV)*

There are two habits that enable us to have the clarity we need to know we are truly moving as God would have us move. We must be in tune with the Spirit through fasting and prayer in order to allow God to order our steps. Once we have peace in our hearts and clarity in our spirit we must walk by faith and not by sight knowing God is guiding us! This takes a deep commitment to prayer before we plan and praying so that we may persevere to the point of manifesting the vision for our businesses.

We must encourage ourselves on a daily basis. People will judge us and our plan and compare us to others and suggest we are on the wrong track. Even worse, we may make these same comparisons and discourage ourselves! We must pray to see ourselves and our circumstances as God sees them. At times, circumstances, believers, or unbelievers will suggest an adjustment in our path. We are wise to listen, pray, and test what we hear. Know that God is always working on perfecting us for His purposes through the journey that is entrepreneurship. Remember that God is after our heart and will provide for our needs as long as we pursue Him.

**Prayer**
*Help me to draw closer to You along this journey so I may better understand who You are and what You are preparing me for.*

# Day 5

## God, family, business. Maintaining that order.

*Better one handful with tranquillity than two handfuls with toil and chasing after the wind.*

*Ecclesiastes 4:6 (NIV)*

The relentless daily grind of being an entrepreneur can become all consuming. Forgetting to make time for prayer and meditation and for our extended families, spouses, and children can compromise everything, including our business. Our Father is our source of energy and strength. In order to prosper, we must remain in sync with Him by taking time daily to commune with Him. Of course, our spouses and children are our responsibility on this earth. We must make it a priority to attend to their needs, love and support them, and be available. We must trust God to give us wisdom and judgment as to how to balance work with family life. We must look to God to supply us with grace and energy to be able to do so. Ignore the foolish people who say we have to work ourselves to death and stay up all night to succeed. Yes, there will be those days and those times, but if we pursue a way of life that leaves God and family on the sidelines we're doing something wrong. We must seek godly counsel and make time for prayer so we can make the adjustments and corrections needed. And always remember the things of this earth that we seek to our obtain are temporary. What we do for our family, how we love and serve them, will truly last into eternity.

**Prayer**
*Lord, help me to keep my priorities in proper order so that I maintain a growing relationship with You, while also honoring my responsibilities to my spouse, family, and business.*

# Day 6

## Being teachable

*In the same way, you who are younger, submit yourselves to your elders. All of you, clothe yourselves with humility toward one another, because, "God opposes the proud but shows favor to the humble."*

*1 Peter 5:5 (NIV)*

Being teachable and knowing whose advice to take is a challenge. We probably ignored a million naysayers to begin our entrepreneurial journeys and we probably continue to ignore some even as we move into some level of success. Even with success, there's always something to learn. There's always new understandings to obtain through the study of the Bible. There is always revelation through the Holy Spirit in our daily lives. There are also people in our lives that God sends to give us instructions on how to improve so that we may be more successful in what God has placed us here to accomplish. It is important in our prayer life to focus on having the right attitude so that we are able to receive. Sometimes receiving instruction will be uncomfortable and even painful. While growth is often painful there is always a blessing on the other side. Maintain the right attitude of heart and understand that our father God is the ultimate teacher.

**Prayer**
*Lord help me to listen and discern, while maintaining a spirit of humility and a focus on You and the work You have put in my hands.*

# Day 7

## Long vision. Small steps.

*Direct my footsteps according to your word; let no sin rule over me.*

*Psalm 119:133 (NIV)*

When we feel as though God has given us a vision, we expect things to happen in short order. This is rarely the case. Often there are many critical and painful steps along the way that must be taken before we can achieve the vision. We must pray that God orders our steps. We must seek to understand God's timing and see our circumstances from a spiritual perspective so that we may act according to His will day in and day out. Remember that God is more concerned with our growth, and growth comes through the pain and challenges of the journey. Stay close to the Father so that our steps may be ordered.

**Prayer**
*Teach me Lord to have patience to continue to work and focus on the details while I wait for You to move on my behalf in Your perfect timing.*

# Day 8

## Along the road less traveled.

*For we live by faith, not by sight.*

*2 Corinthians 5:7 (NIV)*

Along the road less traveled there are many things we will find. At times our path will be smooth. Other times, it will be bumpy. There will be steep hills to climb up and low hills to coast down. There will be roads that are straight, where we can see the horizon far in the distance. The key is to walk by faith not by sight and to stay the course. We may often compare ourselves to others who walk the more common path and are validated. This is when we must realize that our validation and comfort must come from the Father. Seek Him continuously to understand how to proceed along this road. We should not compare ourselves to others. We are unique and so is our journey and purpose.

**Prayer**
*Help me to rely on my relationship with You Father so that I can maintain a spirit of joy and the strength to persevere in all circumstances.*

# Day 9

## Receiving God's Grace

*But by the grace of God I am what I am, and his grace to me was not without effect. No, I worked harder than all of them—yet not I, but the grace of God that was with me.*

*1 Corinthians 15:10 (NIV)*

Learning to receive God's grace, particularly in the midst of disappointments, is critical along our entrepreneurial journey. Negative self talk and self criticism can keep us from finding peace in the presence of God. Negative thoughts and constantly reflecting and holding on to past makes it impossible to receive God's grace. In God's grace, there is renewal and strength. We know we are forgiven for our mistakes and our imperfections. And perhaps most importantly, we come to understand that our imperfections do not have to keep us from what God has for us.

**Prayer**
*Lord, teach me to receive Your grace and to know that my efforts are enough and that You will bridge the gap for us when we don't have the answers or believe we are able.*

# Day 10

## Learning to Recieve

*I have received full payment and have more than enough. I am amply supplied, now that I have received from Epaphroditus the gifts you sent. They are a fragrant offering, an acceptable sacrifice, pleasing to God.*

*Philippians 4:18 (NIV)*

Sometimes we go in to situations with low expectations are are unprepared to receive. Many of us approach an opportunity to serve but are unprepared for our blessing. As an entrepreneur we go to a meeting or presentation prepared to communicate value so that we earn trust and secure a client or partnership. Often, we are so focused on selling the product or service, we are not prepared for what happens when the answer is "yes". If God wishes to bless us; if someone asks us how they can help us or wants to give us an opportunity, how then do we prepare to receive? We must prayerfully request faith and foresight so that we are prepared for opportunity. We can not have an attitude of defeat. Instead, we should have an attitude focused on working towards excellence with an expectation of success. Disciplined preparation and forethought is key. This should be driven by a spirit of humility, openness, and expectation.

**Prayer**
*Father, help me to have an expectant heart that is open to receiving what You have for me. Provide the foresight I need so that I am prepared to receive.*

# Day 11

## Learning to make the ask through prayer. Make the ask by first asking God.

_*"Ask and it will be given to you; seek and you will find; knock and the door will be opened to you. For everyone who asks receives; the one who seeks finds;and to the one who knocks, the door will be opened. Which of you, if your son asks for bread, will give him a stone? Or if he asks for a fish, will give him a snake? If you, then, though you are evil, know how to give good gifts to your children, how much more will your Father in heaven give good gifts to those who ask him!"*

*Matthew 7:7-11 (NIV)*

Making an "ask" for what we want is often one of the most difficult things to do. Whether asking for investment, strategic partnership, grant funding, or making an ask through a client proposal; making an ask is hard! We all struggle with rejection and, of course, if we ask, chances may be we're going to hear "no" more often then we're going to hear "yes". We're blessed to serve a God who often says "yes" and who also says "no". Both of these occur in God infinite wisdom for our benefit. We can overcome this fear by prayerfully asking God to shape our ask and its timing. We can overcome this fear by having the right attitude so that we are ready to properly receive when the answer is yes and to graciously receive a no. And when we get a no, we must trust God and understand it may just mean not yet. Let's challenge ourselves to develop a boldness in asking and watch God bless us in the process! Let's be confident that as a result of our asks, God will bless us beyond what we expected.

### Prayer
*Father, give me the faith to ask for what I want, while also giving me the insight to understand when the answer is "no".*

# Day 12

## Overcoming Fear and Anxiety.

*So do not fear, for I am with you; do not be dismayed, for I am your God. I will strengthen you and help you; I will uphold you with my righteous right hand.*

*Isaiah 41:10 (NIV)*

Fear is not of God. Fear is one of the big biggest obstacles we face and cripples many. Instead of fear, we must turn to the freedom that exists from a relationship with Christ. Our journey as an entrepreneur may often place us in uncomfortable situations. These situations are opportunities for growth in our faith and character. We must be bold in walking out the vision God has given us with the faith to understand he walks with us. Walking out this journey will not always put us in a place of comfort but we cannot allow ourselves to stop because of fear. Instead, let us keep working towards a breakthrough! Apart from God we are subject to anxiety attacks, restless nights, and periods of stress when we think instead of pray. We must consistently and regularly abide in the presence of the Lord. Prayer and fasting are critical. Pray daily knowing that nothing is too big or or too small for God. Let's put our burdens on him. Don't let fear stop us!

**Prayer**
*Lord, help me not to sink into a spirit of fear or depression but instead, help me to be renewed body, mind, and spirit so that I may know who You are and who You see me to be as Your child.*

# Day 13

## The Narrow Gate

*Enter through the narrow gate. For wide is the gate and broad is the road that leads to destruction, and many enter through it. 14 But small is the gate and narrow the road that leads to life, and only a few find it.*

*Matthew 7:13-14 (NIV)*

So often in business life there is the temptation to take shortcuts and sacrifice our values to make more money. It's easy to fall into so many traps, whether it's handling finances, being honest with partners and clients, or giving unto Caesar what is Caesar's. Indeed, the road to success in this world, and freedom in the eyes of God, is narrow. Indeed, we make many sacrifices as an entrepreneur, but one's integrity and faith walk should not be one of them.

**Prayer**
*Help me to understand the difference between acceleration and shortcuts. Help me to not forget to be honest and ethical and law-abiding so that I may honor You by my work.*

# Day 14

## The golden rule.

*So in everything, do to others what you would have them do to you, for this sums up the Law and the Prophets.- Matthew 7:12 (NIV)*

One of the biggest challenges of any entrepreneur and in life in general is managing relationships. How we treat business partners and clients determines many of the outcomes in our business ventures. Our business and work culture often encourages us to do what it takes at all costs, and often to the detriment of our health (physical, mental, spiritual) and family, to succeed. However it is wise for the entrepreneur who can listen to God and operate in his spirit. There's something to be said for maintaining a attitude in proper balance between achieving our goals and maintaining our peace and integrity. No doubt short-term gains can be had by following the world's approach, but there is an eternal gain that we must always keep in mind when we relate to others. We must maintain the spirit of generosity, while also being wise and shrewd. Matthew 10:16 tells us to "[B]e as shrewd as snakes and as innocent as doves." We do not have to be mean and nasty to be successful. We must respond with grace and love as we encounter challenging people and difficult circumstances. We all fall short, so let us remember to apply the grace that we've received.

**Prayer**
Help me to lead in the marketplace with a spirit of love and to treat others as I would want to be treated so that even though I may walk with kings, I do not lose the common touch.

# Day 15

## Putting Our Dream on the Alter

*Trust in the Lord with all your heart and lean not on your own understanding; in all your ways submit to him, and he will make your paths straight.*

*Proverbs 3:5-6 (NIV)*

It's hard to have a vision and trust God to fulfill it. Entrepreneurs are ambitious and we see opportunities to create value or make something better . We're designers. We're thinkers, planners, and doers. But we also have to take the time to step away and pray. We truly have to trust God and give the vision to him to fill in the details and help us walk it out. We have to trust God to bring the resources and necessary correction. We have to trust God to help us improve and be better people. Most importantly, we truly have to know that our journey is a faith walk. We can choose to go our own way but the consequences and an opportunity can pass us by. We have to trust that God has a plan for our lives. And even if things don't end up looking exactly how we initially envisioned, we have to trust that God has positioned us in our best interest and that He will bless and prosper us as we go forward.

**Prayer**
*Every day help me to give my dreams and ambitions to You so that You may perfect them and fulfill them in Your time and for Your purposes. Help me to know that as a result, I will grow closer to You and be blessed while being a blessing.*

# Day 16

## Being obedient in the midst of uncertainty

*Blessed are all who fear the Lord, who walk in obedience to him.*

*Psalm 128:1 (NIV)*

One of our biggest challenges as an entrepreneur is being obedient to the Spirit. Many circumstances challenge us and can result in us responding emotionally and in our own way. We must learn to ask and listen so that we are aligned with the Spirit. Maintaining spiritual alignment is critical. Even when the world says hurry up and decide, sometimes it's best to delay. Sometimes there's strength in silence. Sometimes not responding can simply be our answer. We must be yielded to the Spirit. With mobile technology and the fast pace of the modern world, remaining yielded is one of our biggest challenges. Staying in a place physically and mentally where we can hear from God daily is critical in order to gain and preserve clarity. Gaining clarity gives us the faith and helps us maintain the discipline to obey.

**Prayer**
*Father, help me to have clarity in my direction and to be obedient in making our venture what You'd have it be.*

# Day 17

## Bearing Up Under the Burden

*For my yoke is easy and my burden is light.*

*Matthew 11:30 (NIV)*

We must allow God to bear our burdens. Often, we want to be conquerors, but we forget where our strength lies. Being unwilling to allow God to bear our burdens can take a physical, mental, and spiritual toll on us. As leaders, our responsibilities are substantial and we feel like the fate of our enterprise is all up to us. Because of this, we must remember who the source of our strength is. We must remember who set us out on this journey and what the purpose of the journey is: to make us better and more useful in service to Him. As a result, we will have more love, peace, and joy. And as entrepreneurs, we will see our labor bear fruit.

**Prayer**
*Help me to lean on You Father and to know where my strength lies.*

# Day 18

## When God's no is not yet.

*But those who hope in the Lord will renew their strength. They will soar on wings like eagles; they will run and not grow weary, they will walk and not be faint.*

*Isaiah 40:31 (NIV)*

We think we're ready, but then God says "not yet". We all work hard to see progress on a given project or initiative. We all want to think we're ready for the financial investment in our venture or for the big client. But sometimes, we experience silence or even the appearance of a set back. In these times, we must persist in prayer to understand what is happening in the Spirit. Seek to understand God's perspective. In doing so, we'll be able to get a more objective view of where we are in our journey. How can we proceed to turn that "not yet' into a "yes". When our yes comes it'll often be a lot more than we hoped or ask for. God never gives us more than what we're ready for but when God gives, He tends to do so quite generously. Be persistent and keep walking the walk.

**Prayer**
*Lord, give us the faith and strength to persevere and remain focused on who You are and what You have promised us.*

# Day 19

## Leading with Love

*Love is patient, love is kind. It does not envy, it does not boast, it is not proud. It does not dishonor others, it is not self-seeking, it is not easily angered, it keeps no record of wrongs. Love does not delight in evil but rejoices with the truth. It always protects, always trusts, always hopes, always perseveres. Love never fails.*

*1 Corinthians 13: 4-8 (NIV)*

In popular culture often there are two approaches to leadership that are presented; one in which we are respected, and one in which we are feared. Jesus example in the Bible is clearly different. Jesus gave clear instructions that love empowered his disciples who He then led by example. Fear only gets us so far and while respect is good, it is insufficient. As entrepreneurs we must lead with love so that our relationships can be strong and our example as Christians will shine beyond our success. Prayerfully seek to understand and demonstrate the fruit of the Spirit in all things. Galatians 5:22-23 tell us that *"the fruit of the Spirit is love, joy, peace, forbearance, kindness, goodness, faithfulness, gentleness and self-control."* Seek out examples of servant leadership. We shouldn't consider a task to be above or beneath us in our businesses. The most powerful example of leadership is a leader who is willing to come alongside those who work for, or with us in service.

**Prayer**
*Father, help me to have the courage, whether for profit or not for profit, to lead my enterprise with a spirit of loving service.*

# Day 20

## Pitching with Purpose

*Many are the plans in a person's heart, but it is the Lord's purpose that prevails.*

*Proverbs 19:21 (NIV)*

I love talking about my business and the exciting things we're doing. On the other hand, I hate feeling that often I have to convince a decision-maker or someone who can impact my enterprise's outcome, of something that's so obvious to me. It's hard to communicate our dreams and share our vision and ideas with people, especially when they come from God. Sometimes there are insecurities because we know we don't have all the answers. Whether we're pitching for financing or clients, always be ready to pitch. When we do pitch, do it with a purpose! So what's the purpose? It's simply knowing that the blessings that God will provide us through our enterprises will extend beyond us to our families, the people with whom we partner and those we hire, and to those whose critical needs our companies will meet in the marketplace. We must look to God to have clarity as to our purpose. This purpose may not show up in our pitch materials, but it will show up in our spirit. Enthusiasm and the right attitude will certainly help win the day.

**Prayer**
*Father help me to know my purpose and incorporate it into my attitude so that it is reflected in my execution and personality.*

# Day 21

## Managing Business with Friends And Family

*Do not be yoked together with unbelievers. For what do righteousness and wickedness have in common? Or what fellowship can light have with darkness?*

*2 Corinthians 6:14 (NIV)*

Starting a business with a family member or friend is one of the riskiest things to do. I have spoken to many business leaders who recommend against it but, of course, for so many of us, it's unavoidable. It can be even more difficult if we are not aligned spiritually with our friend or family member. Proceed thoughtfully and prayerfully. We must be prayerful in particular as to our role in the relationship and as to the nature and requirements of the partnership. Computer. I've had a friendship deteriorate into a contentious business relationship when success didn't happen as quickly as expected and the needs and requirements of the business, and people involved, changed. We shouldn't assume because someone is close to us that they share and understand our vision or share our determination to see the venture succeed. We must be sure we are equally yoked in this regard.

**Prayer**
*Lord, help me to be prayerful and to have discernment concerning with whom I partner and share authority in the enterprise You have entrusted me to lead.*

# Day 22

## How to say No and what it means

*The world and its desires pass away, but whoever does the will of God lives forever.*

*1 John 2:17 (NIV)*

Remaining focused as an entrepreneur is difficult, particularly in the early stages of a venture. Identifying tasks and working with a new team on a new project is daunting. As a leader or entrepreneur, we are often approached to contribute to different projects or support the ideas and dreams of others. Saying "no" can be hard to do but, in doing so, we are saying "yes" to focusing on the tasks God has put before us. If believe God is ordering our steps, we will have peace. Sometimes a request will speak to our hearts. We must be prayerful and mindful of our priorities. Distraction is the enemy and so is being unequally yoked. We should use prayer and the priorities we believe God has given us as guideposts when making a decision as to where we invest our time and energy. Stay focused!

**Prayer**
*Father, help me to respond lovingly to all requests while remaining focused on the work You have put in my hands.*

# Day 23

## When to give and when to ask.

*Stay there, eating and drinking whatever they give you, for the worker deserves his wages. Do not move around from house to house.*

*Luke 10:7 (NIV)*

Jesus gave of Himself freely. He gave of His wisdom, time, and power while on earth before making the ultimate sacrifice on the cross. As Christians, we are to model this behavior. As business people however, we know that if we give the store away, we won't succeed. So where, when, and how do we make "the ask" while continuing to model Christ? Unlike Christ, our resources are not limitless. Therefore in order to give and serve, we must receive. Even Christ went to the desert for 40 days to receive from our Father in heaven so that He could continue to give and be prepared to die on the cross. We must define what we can give before we ask our customer, client, or partner to do the same. We must prayerfully seek God to know, and then plan accordingly. There is no science to this. Instead, it's the art of loving people and wanting to improve their lives that should inform our entrepreneurship. If we serve people well, people will give before we even ask and that's an awesome blessing.

**Prayer**
*Father, help me to know when to give and when and how to request my proper wage.*

# Day 24

## The rain drops before the deluge: Preparing for an outpouring

*The person without the Spirit does not accept the things that come from the Spirit of God but considers them foolishness, and cannot understand them because they are discerned only through the Spirit.*

*1 Corinthians 2:14 (NIV)*

There's nothing like a summer storm. First you feel the winds change and you see the clouds coming. Then there are a few rain drops. Soon, there is a deluge and the streets become a river. Often, this is how God works when blessings are coming. First, we may sense the spiritual winds shift. Then we'll see hints or patterns of coming blessings. Finally, there is the outpouring we have waited for. If we had no sense of shifting winds but perhaps noticed a few rain drops, would we have been ready for the outpouring and overflow? Or would we be washed away? The key is to stay alert; learn to recognize the signs, and be prepared. How? By developing our relationship with God so that we may have faith and discern the season we're in.

**Prayer**
*Help me to discern the season I am in and to be prepared for the blessings this season holds for me.*

# Day 25

## Having Peace in Our powerlessness

*And the peace of God, which transcends all understanding, will guard your hearts and your minds in Christ Jesus.*

*Philippians 4:7 (NIV)*

As an entrepreneur, one of the many things we are likely confronted with on a daily basis is just how powerless we are. Many external circumstances beyond our control can impact our businesses. While focus and attention to detail are key factors for success, it's impossible to account for, let alone prepare for, every possibility and variable. When we fall short, or things don't go our way because of something we can't control or, what some refer to as "bad luck" we can end up in a state of depression and despair. This leads us to be sidelined and sidetracked temporarily, if not permanently, which can cause us to miss the growth opportunity in the circumstance and the blessing yet to come. Therefore, we must seek peace in our circumstances and develop a personal knowledge of Who truly has the power to determine our outcomes. We should keep our peace at all cost and understand where and with Whom our power lies.

**Prayer**
*Lord, I pray that You will give me peace and help me to know how to keep it regardless of the circumstance.*

# Day 26

## Mission, not Money Focused

*Man does not live on bread alone but on every word that comes from the mouth of the Lord.*

*Deuteronomy 8:3 (NIV)*

Money is a tool, one of many, that will allow us and our enterprise to achieve its mission. Keeping money and mission in this perspective is key to the success of the enterprise. Of course, entrepreneurs usually need to raise and earn money and continue to do so to sustain the enterprise. But, almost daily in the news, there are many examples of enterprises that have focused on money so much more than mission that they have lied to, endangered, and stolen from customers and employees. In doing so, they have compromised trust and lost clients. Some businesses never recover. By remaining focused on mission and meeting the critical needs of people in the marketplace or in society in general, the idea of money will be kept in proper perspective and in proper relationship to our businesses and our walk with Christ.

**Prayer**
*Father, help me to remain focused on You and the mission You have given me to carry out for my enterprise, while keeping money in proper perspective as a tool to achieve the mission.*

# Day 27

## The Fruit of Forbearance.

*But the fruit of the Spirit is love, joy, peace, forbearance, kindness, goodness, faithfulness...*

*Galatians 5:22*

People are difficult. Loving people is very difficult, but Jesus provides the perfect example of how we can love one another despite ourselves. Forbearance is a word many of us may not use regularly or be familiar with however, it is one of the fruits of the spirit and is defined as "patient self-control; restraint and tolerance." There will be people in our enterprises or whom our enterprise serves that will require a great deal of patience. Many times, we let our preferences, pride, and emotions get the best of us. And on many of those occasions, we may be justified, but we must be careful to not make a mountain out of a molehill. Of course, God moves mountains but, they our attention, work, and prayers focused on moving them. We must persevere in forbearance by learning to see people as God sees them. When we seek that level of understanding, we'll realize often times that we are not the reason a person's attitude has proven challenging. This realization will allow us to stay mission focused and love people by showing restraint.

**Prayer**
*Father, help me to understand how to practice forbearance and to have an attitude of thanks for all the times You and others have practiced forbearance with me.*

# Day 28

## Acknowledging obstacles without giving them power.

*And it will be said: "Build up, build up, prepare the road! Remove the obstacles out of the way of my people."*

*Isaiah 57:14 (NIV)*

Often we will encounter circumstances or relationships that seem to stand in the way of our progress and mission. Often we might over analyze a situation and make it seem worse than it is. Other times, our analysis is spot on and the obstacle is in fact a real problem. We can't ignore the problem but we can not cede to it the power to determine the outcome. The power must come in acknowledging the situation and prayerfully seeking clarity and a solution. We must trust God to either remove the obstacle, change our perspective regarding the obstacle, or show us a way over, around, or through it. We also must seek the lesson and how God could be using this as an opportunity for us to expand our capability, faith, and relationships. Remember who truly has the power. Don't get bogged down and don't give up. We are to press in through prayer to find our next step and keep on stepping.

**Prayer**
*Father, help me to not be discouraged when challenges arise but, instead, help me to seek You for the next move and to know how the obstacle will be overcome.*

# Day 29

## Leveraging the engine of prayer to grow Our enterprises.

*The prayer of a righteous person is powerful and effective.*

*James 5:16*

Learning how to pray into our enterprises for the people, resources, and opportunities to grow our businesses is crucial to understanding where God is taking us and to gaining clarity as to how we will arrive at that place. When we don't know what to pray for, we must quiet ourselves and ask God. Call on Him by name and he will respond. No request is too big or too small. No time is a bad time or the wrong time. I've prayed in bathrooms, in meetings, in the car, and in mid sentence. God knows us and our thoughts intimately. He made us fearfully and wonderfully. Maintaining an ongoing dialogue is key to understanding how He sees us and our circumstances. Once we understand that, we'll be praying into God's will for our lives and our steps will truly be ordered.

**Prayer**
*Father, give me the courage to pray unceasingly, knowing that You are with me and are moving mightily on my behalf and on behalf of my enterprise.*

# Day 30

## We are qualified. (A Challenge)

*1 Samuel 17 (David & Goliath)*

David & Goliath is one my favorite Bible stories and one I reflect on often. Underwhelming in stature, with no apparent skills for the opportunity for which he aspired, David boldly seized the opportunity to slay the giant and win the battle. David wasn't even in the army! What David did have was a unique perspective and a unique skill set. Don't we all? What David also had is what we sometimes lack: faith.

In 1 Samuel 17:34-35, David tells Saul of how he killed the bear who was trying to kill his sheep and that he could do the same thing to the Philistine, Goliath. In verse 37 David tells Saul *"The Lord who rescued me from the paw of the lion and the paw of the bear will rescue me from the hand of this Philistine."* What faith! The Lord had brought him through before, so why would this time be any different? Saul could only say, *"Go, and the Lord be with you."* So this, I say to you: God has brought you through and gotten you to this point in your venture. He has stood by you before and He will again. You are able and you are qualified by the grace of God. So go! And the Lord be with you.

**Prayer**
*Help us to understand our gifts and talents. Help us to know that when they are combined with faith and a relationship with You, amazing things are possible. Help us to know that in You and through You, we are qualified.*

# Biblical Reference

*But seek first his kingdom and his righteousness, and all these things will be given to you as well.*
Matthew 6:33 (NIV) Page 6, Day 1

*Do not be yoked together with unbelievers. For what do righteousness and wickedness have in common? Or what fellowship can light have with darkness? What harmony is there between Christ and Belial ? Or what does a believer have in common with an unbeliever?*
2 Corinthians 6:14-15 (NIV) Page 7, Day 2

*Out of his fullness we have all received grace in place of grace already given.*
John 1:16 (NIV) Page 8, Day 3

*The Lord makes firm the steps*
*of the one who delights in him;*
*though he may stumble, he will not fall,*
*for the Lord upholds him with his hand.*
Psalm 37:23-24 (NIV) Page 9, Day 4

*Better one handful with tranquillity than two handfuls with toil and chasing after the wind.*
Ecclesiastes 4:6 (NIV) Page 10, Day 5

*In the same way, you who are younger, submit yourselves to your elders. All of you, clothe yourselves with humility toward one another, because, "God opposes the proud but shows favor to the humble."*
1 Peter 5:5 (NIV) Page 11, Day 6

*Direct my footsteps according to your word; let no sin rule over me.*
Psalm 119:133 (NIV) Page 12, Day 7

*For we live by faith, not by sight.*
2 Corinthians 5:7 (NIV) Page 13, Day 8

*But by the grace of God I am what I am, and his grace to me
was not without effect. No, I worked harder than all of
them—yet not I, but the grace of God that was with me.
1 Corinthians 15:10 (NIV) Page 14, Day 9*

*I have received full payment and have more than enough. I am
amply supplied, now that I have received from Epaphroditus
the gifts you sent. They are a fragrant offering, an acceptable
sacrifice, pleasing to God.
Philippians 4:18 (NIV) Page 15, Day 10*

*Ask and it will be given to you; seek and you will find; knock
and the door will be opened to you.  For everyone who asks
receives; the one who seeks finds;and to the one who knocks, the
door will be opened. Which of you, if your son asks for bread,
will give him a stone? Or if he asks for a fish, will give him a
snake? If you, then, though you are evil, know how to give good
gifts to your children, how much more will your Father in
heaven give good gifts to those who ask him!
Matthew 7:7-11 (NIV) Page 16, Day 11*

*So do not fear, for I am with you; do not be dismayed, for I am
your God. I will strengthen you and help you; I will uphold you
with my righteous right hand.
Isaiah 41:10 (NIV) Page 17, Day 12*

*Enter through the narrow gate. For wide is the gate and broad
is the road that leads to destruction, and many enter through
it. 14 But small is the gate and narrow the road that leads to
life, and only a few find it.
Matthew 7:13-14 (NIV) Page 18, Day 13*

*So in everything, do to others what you would have them do to
you, for this sums up the Law and the Prophets.- Matthew 7:12
(NIV) Page 19, Day 14*

*Trust in the Lord with all your heart and lean not on your own understanding; in all your ways submit to him, and he will make your paths straight.*
*Proverbs 3:5-6 (NIV), Page 20, Day 15*

*Blessed are all who fear the Lord, who walk in obedience to him.*
*Psalm 128:1 (NIV) Page 21, Day 16*

*For my yoke is easy and my burden is light.*
*Matthew 11:30 (NIV) Page 22, Day 17*

*But those who hope in the Lord will renew their strength. They will soar on wings like eagles; they will run and not grow weary, they will walk and not be faint.*
*Isaiah 40:31 (NIV) Page 23, Day 18*

*Love is patient, love is kind. It does not envy, it does not boast, it is not proud. It does not dishonor others, it is not self-seeking, it is not easily angered, it keeps no record of wrongs. Love does not delight in evil but rejoices with the truth. It always protects, always trusts, always hopes, always perseveres. Love never fails.*
*1 Corinthians 13: 4-8 (NIV) Page 24, Day 19*

*Many are the plans in a person's heart, but it is the Lord's purpose that prevails.*
*Proverbs 19:21 (NIV) Page 25, Day 20*

*Do not be yoked together with unbelievers. For what do righteousness and wickedness have in common? Or what fellowship can light have with darkness?*
*2 Corinthians 6:14 (NIV) Page 26, Day 21*

*The world and its desires pass away, but whoever does the will of God lives forever.*
*1 John 2:17 (NIV) Page 27, Day 22*

*Stay there, eating and drinking whatever they give you, for the worker deserves his wages. Do not move around from house to house.*
*Luke 10:7 (NIV) Page 28, Day 23*

*The person without the Spirit does not accept the things that come from the Spirit of God but considers them foolishness, and cannot understand them because they are discerned only through the Spirit.*
*1 Corinthians 2:14 (NIV) Page 29, Day 24*

*And the peace of God, which transcends all understanding, will guard your hearts and your minds in Christ Jesus.*
*Philippians 4:7 (NIV) Page 30, Day 25*

*Man does not live on bread alone but on every word that comes from the mouth of the Lord.*
*Deuteronomy 8:3 (NIV) Page 31, Day 26*

*But the fruit of the Spirit is love, joy, peace, forbearance, kindness, goodness, faithfulness...*
*Galatians 5:22 (NIV) Page 32, Day 27*

*And it will be said: "Build up, build up, prepare the road! Remove the obstacles out of the way of my people."*
*Isaiah 57:14 (NIV) Page 33, Day 28*

*The prayer of a righteous person is powerful and effective.*
*James 5:16 (NIV) Page 34. Day 29*

*David and Goliath*
*1 Samuel 17 (NIV) Page 35, Day 30*

# 30 Prayers for Entrepreneurs

**Day 1 Prayer**

> Father, help me to know that You are my first and
> most important business partner and that through a
> relationship with You, You will order my steps and see
> to it that my enterprise flourishes unto Your glory.

**Day 2 Prayer**

> Lord, teach me to be discerning in selecting partners in
> my venture and to not be seduced by potential, but,
> instead, seek to prayerfully discern spiritual
> alignment.

**Day 3 Prayer**

> Lord, help me to extend grace to people in the
> marketplace regardless of their affiliation,
> understanding we all ultimately fall short.

**Day 4 Prayer**

> Help me to draw closer to You along this journey so I
> may better understand who You are and what You are
> preparing me for.

**Day 5 Prayer**

> Lord, help me to keep my priorities in proper order so
> that I maintain a growing relationship with You, while
> also honoring my responsibilities to my spouse, family,
> and business.

**Day 6 Prayer**

> Lord help me to listen and discern, while maintaining
> a spirit of humility and a focus on You and the work
> You have put in my hands.

**Day 7 Prayer**

*Teach me Lord to have patience to continue to work and focus on the details while I wait for You to move on my behalf in Your perfect timing.*

**Day 8 Prayer**

*Help me to rely on my relationship with You Father so that I can maintain a spirit of joy and the strength to persevere in all circumstances.*

**Day 9 Prayer**

*Lord, teach me to receive Your grace and to know that my efforts are enough and that You will bridge the gap for us when we don't have the answers or believe we are able.*

**Day 10 Prayer**

*Father, help me to have an expectant heart that is open to receiving what You have for me. Provide the foresight I need so that I am prepared to receive.*

**Day 11 Prayer**

*Father, give me the faith to ask for what I want, while also giving me the insight to understand when the answer is "no".*

**Day 12 Prayer**

*Lord, help me not to sink into a spirit of fear or depression but instead, help me to be renewed body, mind, and spirit so that I may know who You are and who You see me to be as Your child.*

**Day 13 Prayer**

*Help me to understand the difference between acceleration and short cuts. Help me to not forget to be honest and ethical and law-abiding so that I may honor You by my work.*

### Day 14 Prayer

*Help me to lead in the marketplace with a spirit of love and to treat others as I would want to be treated so that even though I may walk with kings, I do not lose the common touch.*

### Day 15 Prayer

*Every day help me to give my dreams and ambitions to You so that You may perfect them and fulfill them in Your time and for Your purposes. Help me to know that as a result, I will grow closer to You and be blessed while being a blessing.*

### Day 16 Prayer

*Father, help me to have clarity in my direction and to be obedient in making our venture what You'd have it be.*

### Day 17 Prayer

*Help me to lean on You Father and to know where my strength lies.*

### Day 18 Prayer

*Lord, give us the faith and strength to persevere and remain focused on who You are and what You have promised us.*

### Day 19 Prayer

*Father, help me to have the courage, whether for profit or not for profit, to lead my enterprise with a spirit of loving service.*

### Day 20 Prayer

*Father help me to know my purpose and incorporate it into my attitude so that it is reflected in my execution and personality.*

### Day 21 Prayer

*Lord, help me to be prayerful and to have discernment concerning with whom I partner and share authority in the enterprise You have entrusted me to lead.*

### Day 22 Prayer

*Father, help me to respond lovingly to all requests while remaining focused on the work You have put in my hands.*

### Day 23 Prayer

*Father, help me to know when to give and when and how to request my proper wage.*

### Day 24 Prayer

*Help me to discern the season I am in and to be prepared for the blessings this season holds for me.*

### Day 25 Prayer

*Lord, I pray that You will give me peace and help me to know how to keep it regardless of the circumstance.*

### Day 26 Prayer

*Father, help me to remain focused on You and the mission You have given me to carry out for my enterprise, while keeping money in proper perspective as a tool to achieve the mission.*

### Day 27 Prayer

*Father, help me to understand how to practice forbearance and to have an attitude of thanks for all the times You and others have practiced forbearance with me.*

### Day 28 Prayer

*Father, help me to not be discouraged when challenges arise but, instead, help me to seek You for the next move and to know how the obstacle will be overcome.*

### Day 29 Prayer

*Father, give me the courage to pray unceasingly, knowing that You are with me and are moving mightily on my behalf and on behalf of my enterprise.*

### Day 30 Prayer

*Help us to understand our gifts and talents. Help us to know that when they are combined with faith and a relationship with You, amazing things are possible. Help us to know that in You and through You, we are qualified.*

Visit www.RussellFugett.com to contact him for speaking engagements, listen & subscribe to the podcast, read the blog, and learn about current and future projects.


Visit www.GoodWordDigital.com to learn about Russell's business ventures and professional services.

www.ingramcontent.com/pod-product-compliance
Lightning Source LLC
Chambersburg PA
CBHW030538220526
45463CB00007B/2881